GREAT MINECRAFT® BUILDS

YOUR UNOFFICIAL GUIDE TO BUILDING COOL MINECRAFT® SKYSCRAPERS

S. D. MORISON

Enslow PUBLISHING

Please visit our website, www.enslow.com. For a free color catalog of all our high-quality books, call toll free 1-800-398-2504 or fax 1-877-980-4454.

Library of Congress Cataloging-in-Publication Data
Names: Morison, S. D., author.
Title: Your unofficial guide to building cool Minecraft® skyscrapers / S.D. Morison.
Description: New York : Enslow Publishing, 2023. | Series: Great Minecraft builds | Includes index.
Identifiers: LCCN 2022005778 (print) | LCCN 2022005779 (ebook) | ISBN 9781978529403 (library binding) | ISBN 9781978529380 (paperback) | ISBN 9781978529397 (set) | ISBN 9781978529410 (ebook)
Subjects: LCSH: Minecraft (Game)–Juvenile literature. | Skyscrapers–Juvenile literature.
Classification: LCC GV1469.35.M535 M673 2023 (print) | LCC GV1469.35.M535 (ebook) | DDC 794.8/5–dc23/eng/20220209
LC record available at https://lccn.loc.gov/2022005778
LC ebook record available at https://lccn.loc.gov/2022005779

Published in 2023 by
Enslow Publishing
29 E. 21st Street
New York, NY 10010

Portions of this work were originally authored by Ryan Nagelhout and published as *The Unofficial Guide to Building Skyscrapers in Minecraft.* All new material this edition authored by S. D. Morison.

Designer: Rachel Rising
Editor: Jill Keppeler
Illustrator: Matías Lapegüe

Photo credits: Cover, pp. 1-4, 6, 8, 10, 12, 14, 16, 18, 20, 22-24 Orange Sky ART/Shutterstock.com; Cover, pp. 1-24 Phoenix 1319/Shutterstock.com; Cover, pp. 1, 3, 6, 8, 10, 12, 14, 16, 18, 22-24 Soloma/Shutterstock.com; p. 4 Songquan Deng/Shutterstock.com; pp. 6, 8, 10, 12, 14, 16, 18 Phoenix 1319/Shutterstock.com; p. 7 Photogeratphy/Shutterstock.com; p. 15 pinholeimaging/Shutterstock.com; p. 19 Azril Mansor/Shutterstock.com.

Printed in the United States of America

CPSIA compliance information: Batch #CSENS23: For further information contact Enslow Publishing, New York, New York, at 1-800-398-2504.

CONTENTS

Words in the glossary appear in **bold** type the first time they are used in the text.

EARTH BELOW, SKY ABOVE

A *Minecraft* world reaches very deep underground, where you can find many **resources** and interesting things. It also reaches far up into the sky! You can create buildings on the surface to house you and your possessions.

These buildings can be small and basic—or they can be huge and tall! You can build skyscrapers that reach up to the clouds. And if you build a number of them together with smaller buildings, you can make a *Minecraft* city! It can be **fantastic** or **realistic**—or a mix of both. It's all up to you.

In the real world, you can't build skyscrapers with **materials** such as emerald or diamond. In *Minecraft*, you can!

SURVIVE AND CREATE

A number of things in *Minecraft* will affect how hard it will be to build skyscrapers—or any buildings, really! One important **detail** is whether you play in survival mode or creative mode. In survival mode, you'll have to hunt down and collect all the things you need for your buildings. At the same time, you'll need to eat and avoid or fight monsters.

However, if you play in creative mode, building is much easier. You can fly, and you'll have an endless supply of every block in the game to use right away.

ADVENTURE MODE

It takes nine iron ingots, or bricks, (or nine diamonds, emeralds, etc.) to make a block of that material in *Minecraft*. Imagine how many you'd need for a skyscraper!

A *Minecraft* world stretches from -64 blocks deep underground to 319 blocks into the sky. Clouds form between block levels 192 and 196.

MANY MATERIALS

If you've seen real-life skyscrapers in person or in pictures, you can probably guess that they're often made of metal and glass. Metals in *Minecraft* include iron, copper, and gold. Glass comes in blocks or sheets called panes. You can usually see through glass, but you can also **dye** it different colors or **tint** it so it blocks light.

Of course, you can use fancier materials such as diamond or amethyst for your skyscrapers too. Or you can use materials such as terra-cotta or concrete, both of which come in many colors.

ADVENTURE MODE

***Minecraft* copper comes in different forms, including plain blocks of copper and blocks of cut copper. Copper turns greenish over time unless you use a piece of honeycomb to make it waxed copper.**

In the real world, a skyscraper is generally considered to be a building that's at least 492 feet (150 m) tall.

SO MUCH STONE

If you decide you just want to build with stone, you still have many choices. The game has plain, smooth gray stone blocks, cobblestone, stone bricks, sandstone, red sandstone, dripstone, andesite, granite, diorite, obsidian, tuff, and deepslate—and different varieties of many of these as well! Prismarine and dark prismarine are types of stone you can only find underwater.

In the dangerous area called the Nether, you can find glowstone (which gives off light), blackstone, and basalt, as well as varieties of these. In the End region, you can find yellowish end stone.

ADVENTURE MODE

You can use bedrock to build in creative mode, but in survival, it's so hard you can't even mine it! You can find it at the very deepest level of a *Minecraft* world.

BLACKSTONE

Stone is the most common natural block in *Minecraft*. Other common blocks are sand, gravel, wood, and dirt blocks.

CUT COPPER

DEEPSLATE BRICKS

SAFETY FIRST

People called architects **design** skyscrapers in the real world. They have to know how to build a skyscraper safely. Very tall buildings must have a very strong base to hold their weight and help them **resist** the force of **gravity**.

You don't have to worry about gravity much in *Minecraft*. Most blocks aren't affected by it. If you're playing in survival mode, however, you'll have to be careful about gravity's effect on *you*. You can fall up to three blocks without hurting yourself. After that, you'll lose half a heart of fall damage for every block fallen.

ADVENTURE MODE

Sand, red sand, concrete powder, and gravel are the most common blocks affected by gravity in *Minecraft*.

Some *Minecraft* blocks, such as glowstone, sea lanterns, and shroomlight blocks, give off light, and you can use that for some interesting effects.

DECISIONS, DECISIONS

You'll have to decide if your skyscraper is going to be just for show or if you want to use it as a home or base. If it's just for show, you don't even have to put a door in it! You can just **focus** on the outside.

If you do want player characters or mobs to enter the building, you'll need at least one door for entry. Each level needs to be at least two blocks tall. Player characters are 1.8 blocks tall. Villagers are 1.9 to 1.95 blocks tall.

ADVENTURE MODE

Make sure you have plenty of light inside your skyscraper if you plan to use it in survival mode at all. Monsters will spawn in dark places!

Levels inside your skyscraper don't have to be only two blocks tall. You can make them much taller and airier! You can add glass walls so you can see the view.

STURDY STRUCTURE

If you're using your skyscraper as a base, you'll want it to stand up to whatever *Minecraft* mobs (or other players) can throw at it! Use glass instead of open windows so monsters like skeletons can't shoot arrows inside.

Each material also has a different blast resistance. This is how well it holds up to **explosions**. For example, glass has a very low blast resistance of 0.3, while cobblestone has a blast resistance of 6. Obsidian has a blast resistance of 1,200. Bedrock has a blast resistance of 3.6 million!

ADVENTURE MODE

A few things in *Minecraft* can cause explosions. The most famous, however, is probably the monster called a creeper.

A skyscraper waterfall in the real world would probably cause a lot of problems. However, you can build one in *Minecraft*.

WIND AND WEATHER

Real-life skyscrapers also must be able to stand up to another force—that of the wind. Wind forces increase the higher you go. Skyscrapers must have some **flexibility** to move with the air.

You don't need to worry about wind in *Minecraft*. However, there is weather, including snow, rain, and storms. During storms, there's thunder and lightning. If lightning hits your skyscraper, it could burn, and the fire could spread. Avoid using materials such as wood, wool, or coal blocks to build. You can also use a lightning rod to draw lightning away.

ADVENTURE MODE

You can make a lightning rod out of three copper ingots. A lightning rod will draw lightning away from a certain area around it.

In the real world, skyscrapers may also have lightning rods. These are placed on top of the building and include wires to lead the electricity safely to the ground.

REALISTIC OR FANTASTIC

Maybe you want your *Minecraft* skyscrapers to look like real skyscrapers. If so, try to use some of the rules that architects follow to make the real ones. Use a strong foundation, a metal frame, more than a few floors, and many windows. Add a tall point, which is called a spire. Look at buildings in your own community to get ideas.

Or maybe you don't want something realistic at all! You can use all sorts of different shapes and materials to make your skyscrapers. Add gardens in the air or a rainbow of colors. The sky's the limit!

You can even add an elevator to your *Minecraft* building. Try using redstone dust to power a moving platform, or area.

GLOSSARY

design To create the pattern or shape of something. Also, the pattern or shape of something.

detail A small part of something.

dye To add color to something. Also, the material used.

explosion A sudden release of energy.

fantastic Strange, unusual, or unlikely. Not realistic.

flexibility The ability to bend or change easily.

focus To direct attention at something.

gravity The force that pulls objects toward the center of a planet or star. The force that pulls objects toward Earth's center.

material Matter from which something is made.

realistic Based on what is real.

resist To remain strong against the force of something.

resource Something that can be used.

spawn In a video game, to appear or cause something to appear.

tint To give a small amount of color to.

FOR MORE INFORMATION

BOOKS

Guthals, Sarah. *Building a Minecraft City: Build Like a Pro.* Hoboken, New Jersey: John Wiley & Sons Inc, 2018.

Mortimer Children's Books. *Minecraft Master Builder: Ancient Wonders.* London, England: Mortimer, 2021.

Rooney, Anne. *Minecraft Master Builder: Mega Metropolis.* London, England: Mortimer, 2020.

WEBSITES

Awesome 8 Skyscrapers
kids.nationalgeographic.com/awesome-8/article/skyscrapers
This National Geographic Kids website highlights some of the coolest skyscrapers on Earth.

Minecraft: Touch the Sky
www.minecraft.net/de-de/article/touch-sky
The official *Minecraft* website showcases some amazing skyscraper builds.

Tutorials: Best Building Materials
minecraft.fandom.com/wiki/Tutorials/Best_building_materials
The *Minecraft* wiki offers a tutorial on the best building materials to use.

Publisher's note to educators and parents: Our editors have carefully reviewed these websites to ensure that they are suitable for students. Many websites change frequently, however, and we cannot guarantee that a site's future contents will continue to meet our high standards of quality and educational value. Be advised that students should be closely supervised whenever they access the internet.

INDEX